INSIDE THESE WALLS

PRAISE FOR EMILY JAMES

There are those who make survival an art form, and Emily James is a master of her craft. "Inside These Walls" is her story of survival. Told through the lens of poetry and prose, it's a stunning testament to the strength of one woman against all odds. Emily James wields her pen like a razor blade, cutting a trail of light through the darkness within.

—Mandy Kocsis author of Soul Survivor

Emily James balances light and dark beautifully. You can feel her words from the depths of her soul. She strips herself down, revealing her vulnerability as well as her strength with every drop of ink spilled. "I feel hard, I love harder" is one of my favorites quotes by her. I feel the power in the quote. Emily's book "Inside These Walls" is a must have for any poetry lover.

—April Spellmeyer author of Poetry Stained Lips, Scars of a Warrior, and Sacrifice & Bloom

I could sit in front of a fire and cozy up with her writing any day. Truly a beautiful and talented writer.

—Sherri-Lee (Rise of my Fall) author of Moon and Star

I've read her words, and now I know when she speaks it's time to listen.

—Michael McCaffrey (michael_scotts_poetry Instagram)

Emily James is a heartfelt writer who knows how to get to the "heart of the matter." She feels her readers and that in itself is what makes her the writer she is. Knowing what to say and when is not an easy task and Emily has a way of always knowing what needs to be heard at just the right time. Her insight, determination, and passion is shown in all of her work. I have the utmost respect and love for Emily. Keep doing what you are doing always.

—Robin Leah - SobrietyMom

Emily James is a modern poet with an ancient, classical soul. She adds incredible depth to everything she writes. Emily is a multi-talented author that is capable of addressing many multiple subjects. Not only is she able to surface a sense of deep agony from her soul, she is also her own catalyst to a whole world of healing, bravery and undying strength. She displays a delicious array of both light and darkness. An inspiration for our current generation, for many years to come.

—S.A. Quinoxx author of Immortalis, and Tales of Lacrimosa

It's hard to know where to begin when describing the talent of Emily James; she harnesses the power of human emotion, addresses struggles, and shines a light on finding inner strength and overcoming obstacles. Her words provide hope in a very dark world and leave us feeling a little less alone. "Inside These Walls" is a must have for anyone yearning to feel understood."

—Charlene Ann Benoit, author of Fairy Tales & Other Things I Tell Myself

Emily James

INSIDE THESE WALLS

a collection of poetry, prose & deep thoughts

300 SOUTH MEDIA GROUP

NEW YORK

ISBN-13: 978-0-9970356-8-1

First Printing OCTOBER 2021

Front Cover & Book Design by 300 South Media Group

Published by 300 South Media Group | 300smg.com

INTRODUCTION

Welcome to my mind. This is it, the good, the bad, the ugly. This collection contains a little of this and even more of that. That's how my mind works. It never stays in one direction. It would rather run all over the place screaming just to get the full experience.

I have felt every single piece in this book, whether it was my own life experience or from someone I encountered during my journey.

If you have touched my life in any way, good or bad, you live inside these pages. Thank you for giving my words a home. I have met some pretty amazing people walking this path, and I am thankful for each and every one of you.

Emily James

For my Kirsten Nicole

My pride—My joy—My reason

You are my sunshine

Inside these walls
lives a child who never got to be
One who watches life from the corner
She's too afraid to move

There also lives a young girl
She's scared to be alone
The world is changing faster
than she can adapt to it
She can't keep up
Her grip is slipping

Inside these walls
there's a woman who tries to protect them both
The battles have made her strong
She wears her scars with pride
She runs straight towards her demons
as the war rages
Inside these walls

I reached for you in this darkness
Only to find emptiness
I fight these battles alone
The weight of the world
causing my shoulders to ache
I can see the light
I can feel the warmth
I just can't seem to get there

You are a mirror
Whatever you see, you become
An illusion
I see through you
I see through everything you pretend to be
I see what you are
when you think no one is watching
I know your secrets
You keep the real you
locked up tight behind closed doors
I found the key

◇◆◇ ━━━━━ ∘ ♣ ∘ ━━━━━ ◇◆◇

I thought I needed you to live
I was wrong
I needed the woman who watched me from the mirror
The woman I constantly let down
I put her last in every situation
I put her down
I sent her to bed sad
Letting her believe she wasn't enough
Wasn't worth the kind of love she so freely gave
Year after year of torment
Year after year of pain
When things got tough
She was the online one that stayed
The only one I could depend on
When I fell, she picked me up
She was there when life forced me to start over
She made me try harder
She never let me give up
She is me
I am her

◇◆◇ ——————— ◦ ✤ ◦ ——————— ◇◆◇

In your arms, I feel magic
Your love--the most beautiful song
I hear your heart softly beating
My soul dances and sings along

I want to know forever
I've always been the temporary person
The quiet one
The wallflower
The unseen
People come, but they never stay
Temporary emotions
Temporary happiness
Temporary love
The only thing that seems to be forever
is the pain

Remember me
When the sun is starting to set
When the waves have finally calmed
When I can no longer fight this battle
Remember me

No one can see it
I've hidden it well
The dark part inside of me
The part where sadness dwells

I cry my tears in silence
Behind my smile, I hide the pain
My mind is left to wander
Will I ever feel whole again?

How do you survive
in a house that's not a home?
You've planted the seeds
But the love hasn't grown

What do you do
when the world starts to fade?
trying so hard to hold on,
you feel yourself slipping away

Where do you go
When there's nowhere left to hide?
You bury all the shame
You continue living the lie

Demons on her shoulder
WHISPERED
The darkness in her eyes
FLICKERED
She had awakened

◇◆◇ ——————— ∘ ✿ ∘ ——————— ◇◆◇

I said goodbye to a past I can't change
A childhood I couldn't control
I let go of the memories
of a love gone wrong

Today I found myself
I free the woman
I buried years ago
The woman I was
She was patiently waiting for me
Just on the other side of fear

◇◆◇ ——————— ∘ ✿ ∘ ——————— ◇◆◇

You're my one in a million
My saving grace
Your face is what I picture
to escape the reality
of this place

◇◆◇ ▬▬▬▬ ∘ ♣ ∘ ▬▬▬▬ ◇◆◇

He's my little slice of heaven
I'm his reminder
that hell does exist.

◇◆◇ ▬▬▬▬ ∘ ♣ ∘ ▬▬▬▬ ◇◆◇

In a world
where tomorrow is never promised
I will cherish every one of our todays

The only thing she truly wanted
was to be loved
for the woman she wasn't

While they get the best of you
She's alone in the shadows
trying to find love in what's left

You can go cry yourself a river
Go and preach about my sins
Your truths are pure illusions
In my story, Karma always wins

I'm here to show you
a person can have faith
and still question
A heart can be broken
and still love
A soul can be tired
and still hope
A mind can be dark
and still dream
I'm here to show you
that different is beautiful

I'll fight these demons
I'll rise above this pain
I'll walk through life
proudly wearing these scars
If you'll meet me
in the promised land

I hope in some way
I've touched your life
I hope I made you feel safe
I hope I made you feel loved

I hope I have shown you
that the world still has some good in it
That there is some softness left

I hope at the end of the day
you realize you made a difference
and that you are loved

You found such joy
in grounding me
Never letting me fly
Your insecurities
kept my wings clipped

What you didn't know
was clipped wings regrow
The little girl you left behind
grew into a woman
And this woman
you'll never know

◇◆◇ ——————— ∘ ♣ ∘ ——————— ◇◆◇

They call her the Queen of daydreams
Never letting her feet touch the ground
She chased the sun
and kissed the moon goodnight
Never letting life get her down

When sadness is
met with silence
the heart softly shatters

I haven't been myself lately
My heart has been so heavy
I need to cry
but the tears won't come
My mind won't stop
My soul is numb
With every sunrise
I pray for a better day
and when the sun sets
I know more of me has faded away
I don't know how to fix this
I'm not sure what to do
They say all storms will eventually end
but I'm questioning that
is that really true?

◇◆◇ ━━━━━ ∘ ♣ ∘ ━━━━━ ◇◆◇

I tried to love you
With every piece of my broken heart
I tried
Did you enjoy using the pieces
to cut out what was left of my soul?

Everything I learned
about self-hatred
I was taught by
hands that loved me

Forgive me, Father, for I have sinned
I shared a dance with the devil
I fell from grace
He whispered his lies in my ear
He loved too little
and took too much
I stood back and fanned his flames
Against me, he used my every fear
I will never be the same
My innocence is gone
I will wait for your forgiveness
I will wait...
No matter how long

◇◆◇ ──────── ◦ ♣ ◦ ──────── ◇◆◇

I don't think I was meant
for a happily ever after
I see no messages
written in the stars
No fairytale to believe in
No Prince Charming is coming to save me
Love has left me empty-handed
It has left my heart hardened
I would rather walk this journey alone
than risk what little I have left
I know I wouldn't survive another round

I used to think I was too broken for normal
That I was too damaged
but then I found myself
I learned to love myself
and I realized normal isn't what I wanted
I didn't want to get stuck in normal
I need excitement
I crave adventure
I want to get so caught up in living life
that I don't remember what's normal
and my broken past is just a memory

I knew it was time
I knew I had to walk away
We turned into you
Us became you
I knew, in order to save myself
I had to become just me

Some days I get quiet
My soul is screaming
My heart is breaking
I get lost inside my mind
The things I need to say
the world wouldn't understand
I am so lonely
but yet I know I need to be alone

Sometimes you have to let them fly
Even if that means they take a fall

Life isn't always easy
Some days you win
Some days you lose it all

If you are going to love me
Love me loud

If you can't match my passion
Please don't fan my flame

One life, one chance
Step out of the shadows
Let the fire inside you dance

You let your true colors run free
Forgetting I'm not color blind

A leopard doesn't change its spots
It adjusts the mask

The child I never
got to be
weeps for the woman
I am becoming

You were busy
trying to save the world
Always someone's hero
You forgot
you should have been mine
And in that, my darkest hour
I saw just how bright
my soul could shine

You went from my hero
to my nightmare
Claiming you danced in darkness
but you only stumbled
in shades of gray

The dreamer in me
Fell in love with the adventure in you

While you were caught
up in the dream of oleander
the wallflower bloomed

Melancholy madness
It seeps from her soul
Tired of fighting
Tired of trying
She let the darkness
Swallow her whole

I wish I could fly away
I'd fly straight into the dawn
I would rise again with the sun
Find my strength in being reborn

If I could be anything in this word
I'd be your kind of beautiful

*When I'm asked who I want to be
the answer is simple
Her—I wanted to be her
The one that has your heart
While I just share your bed*

*I wish you would look at me
the way you looked at her*

*The smile that crosses your lips
when those memories
flood your mind*

*Maybe another life
Maybe another time*

I've never been much to look at
Kind of a plain type Mary Jane
I don't have long legs
Or a flat stomach
But I'm a woman just the same

My hair has found some silver
My lines are a bit more defined
But never underestimate me
I am a woman in my prime

To write, you have to feel
To feel you have to live
To live, you have to love
and to love,
You have to risk it all

One day I will run out of tomorrows
I won't wake to greet the dawn
I won't witness another sunset
Waves will no longer crash my shore
All I'll be is a memory
Buried deep inside your mind
I hope a smile graces your lips
When you think of me from time to time

Life is changing
I am changing
I am not the same as I was a year ago
I am not the same as I was yesterday
I am wiser
Or maybe I just hope I am
The pains of my past have left scars
Some are still healing
Some are forgotten
People have come and gone
Some I miss, others I don't
I have loved and lost then loved again
My hair is slowly changing to gray
My skin is starting to age
Both are signs that I am alive
That I have survived
My heart may be the only thing
about me that hasn't changed
No matter how many times it has been broken
It still loves and loves deeply
They couldn't take that from me
They never will

My life has always been
a raging storm
           until her
She is my rainbow

When I miss you the most
I go to where the wind whispers
           your name

I am a woman
a daughter, a sister
a mother, a grandmother
I am too much for some
Not enough for others
I have loved too much
and forgave too often
I have been left behind and forgotten
I've cried myself to sleep
then woke up to face the day
I'm the black sheep
The quiet one
The odd girl out
I have known success
I have known failure
I have unfairly judged
and I have been judged
I drive too fast
I work too much
I find beauty in the darkness
I have been a lot of things
but the one thing I will always be
is me

◇◆◇ ———————— ◦ ✤ ◦ ———————— ◇◆◇

I want to love you
under the summer's pink sky
Share kisses
in the cool autumn rain
Let's hold on a little tighter
in the wicked winds of winter
And in the spring
Let's start this all over again

I beat to my own drum
Constantly pounding
through halls of
empty darkness

I've been lost
and I've been found
Then my soul would
wander off again
Many times I've circled
the edge of madness
Only for life to find me again

Just an average nobody
Lost in a raging sea of somebodies
Trying to find a way out

Today with one foot
in my tomorrow
I said goodbye
to my yesterday

So it begins
The cool breeze of autumn
The winds of change
Blowing the sleep from my eyes
The past from my heart
I'm beginning to awaken again

I can't fight this battle alone
I'm not even sure what I'm fighting for
I can't carry the weight of the world
The only thing I hear is the echo
of life slamming the door

We used to be so happy
I used to be your only one
Where a heart goes to rest
when the mind
knows the soul is done?

You look for faults in my life
to hide the dysfunction
in your own

◇◆◇ ══════ ○ ✿ ○ ══════ ◇◆◇

With flowers in her hair
and music in her soul
She was finally free
There was beauty in watching her grow
Watching her bloom
into the woman she was
always meant to be

◇◆◇ ══════ ○ ✿ ○ ══════ ◇◆◇

Meet me
Where the waterfalls are in love with the rocks
Where fairytales do exist and time stands still
Meet me there
and promise me forever

Drinking tea with dysfunction
Doesn't make it a party

Tonight I will find peace
in the darkness
I will forgive myself
Tonight I will have deep conversations
with the moon

Their attention fed your ego
While your love starved my soul

My soul burns for you
Like the raging fires of hell
Claiming the long lost souls
of the damned

Screams from a mind
that can't cope
won't silence the unsteady
beat of my heart
Cries from the childhood
that never was
echo from room to room
Sleep never comes

You don't realize
just how fast time flies
until the only things running through the halls
are memories

◇◆◇ ━━━━━━ ∘ ♣ ∘ ━━━━━━ ◇◆◇

Just remember
When you sell your soul
Karma doesn't offer a refund

◇◆◇ ━━━━━━ ∘ ♣ ∘ ━━━━━━ ◇◆◇

You lost her
While you were busy trying to save the world
She slipped right through your fingers

She needed you
but you wanted them

You were too busy looking for perfection
to notice just how perfect she was

And now it's too late
One day she will move on
and she will
light up someone else's sky

◇◆◇ —————— ○ ✤ ○ —————— ◇◆◇

Some days I forget
I forget that I'm strong
I don't remember how powerful I am
I forget I'm beautiful
Regardless of what you think
I forget what I'm capable of
and I don't remember my own worth

Some days I forget
But God help you
on the days I remember

A single blackbird
Glistening white snow
The memories take over
The tears start to flow
I go back to that place
The place where darkness thrives
I had given up hope
I was waiting to die
You could have saved me
You should have been the one
You fed me lie after lie
Handed me a loaded gun
You almost had it
Victory was in your sights
Blinded by arrogance
You never saw it coming
The phoenix in her rising
Rising strong
from her darkest night

◇◆◇ ━━━━━ ◦ ♣ ◦ ━━━━━ ◇◆◇

I'm not sunshine and rainbows
I'm not pink bows and perfume
In my mind, there's a madness
In my soul, darkness looms

You have to accept who you are
Acknowledge who you were
and be open to who you are becoming
If you want to survive

You are the sweetest melody
Playing over and over in my mind
Dancing under the silver moon
Forever and always
No sense of time

◇◆◇ ━━━━━ ∘ ❖ ∘ ━━━━━ ◇◆◇

I found strength
You found me
Love found us

◇◆◇ ━━━━━ ∘ ❖ ∘ ━━━━━ ◇◆◇

I will not be defined
by your lack of respect
Just like you
will never forget
how my absence feels

◇◆◇ ━━━━━ ○ ✤ ○ ━━━━━ ◇◆◇

Faded pictures
They show a smile I never see
A part of you kept hidden away
Are you lost in there;
deep inside your mind?
Did she take the best of you?
Am I left with the ruins
she left behind?

◇◆◇ ━━━━━ ○ ✤ ○ ━━━━━ ◇◆◇

I am not your option
I'm not your maybe
or when you have the time
I'm not a backup plan
I will not be your secret

You want me to
hand feed your ego
whenever life beats you down
But you let me starve
saving all your love for the masses

I'm done fighting for a spot
When the wind blows
and life leaves you
cold and hungry
Warm yourself on that back burner
I don't use it anymore

◇◆◇ ━━━━━ ∘ ♣ ∘ ━━━━━ ◇◆◇

You haunt me
All the things you never said
The plans we had
They are just places
that we will never see
I miss the sound of your laughter
but not the pain of your touch
You're not the man I thought you were
You're the monster
that every child tries not to dream about

Melancholy madness
It eats me alive
Too old to fight it
Too young to die

And there she stood
Beautifully strong
among those that tried to break her

How long does a soul scream
before the mind finally breaks?

I'm searching for answers
in a world that doesn't
want you asking questions.
They don't want you to understand
They just want you to follow
Nothing more than a number
A faceless body
meant to sacrifice for the common goal

As parents, we think we have more time
There's always the next game
The next concert
The next recital
We think we will always have tomorrow
We'll read that story tomorrow
We'll make that tomorrow, we'll go tomorrow
and there will always be another tomorrow
But today is it
There won't be another today
Someday tomorrow won't matter
because your today is quiet
No more will the door open to loud music
No more laundry piles in the corner
No more collecting dishes from a bedroom
that resembles a war zone
No more first days of school
or lunches to pack
No more
In the blink of an eye, that chapter is done
Your life is different
We become grandparents with this knowledge
So yes, we may spoil a little too much
We may ask for too many visits
and give too many snacks
We have learned the value of every little giggle

There can never be enough little hugs
We don't mind messy faces
and little messy hands
We know that tomorrows fly by
So we savor every single today

I could walk away
but then what?
Live a lie
and pretend I feel no pain?
Tell people I'm fine
when deep inside my soul aches?
Do I spend every night
listening to your voice
play over and over in my mind?
Reliving the memories we made,
do I finish this journey alone
then look for you in our next lifetime,
hoping you learned how to love by then?

◇◆◇ ━━━━ ∘ ♣ ∘ ━━━━ ◇◆◇

When tomorrow doesn't come for me
Please don't bury me deep below
I've spent too many years
already in a box
Set my soul free to finally roam

Take a little piece of me with you
Up into the mountains
Wherever you go
I will always be right beside you
Your love is my forever home

I lost myself
in the opinion of a mad man
With every word he said
Parts of me died

I lost sleep
over words spoken by a coward
His insecurities projecting outward
Spewing hate on those
only trying to love him

I stopped seeing myself
I hid in the shadows
There I tried to protect all I had left
Sacrificing myself
for the sake of silence

◇◆◇ ———— ○ ✣ ○ ———— ◇◆◇

I have lived in the dark
for so long
I forgot
What the sun felt like

I sat in the shadows
instead of chasing my dreams

I got so caught up
in what I was supposed to be
that I forgot who I was

It took almost losing my mind
to remember
but I did remember
I no longer call the shadows home

◇◆◇ ——————— ○ ✿ ○ ——————— ◇◆◇

Her soul
will shine brighter
than your bullshit ever will

The girl who hid her broken wings
grew into the woman who learned to fly
And fly she did

Wisps of your hair
catching the morning light
Patiently waiting
for your first cup of coffee
Little reminders of last night's slumber
still in your eyes
—I love you most

When you've had a long day
You're tired and worn
You've worked hard, and it shows
—I love you most

When you don't know I'm watching
the faint smile on your lips
the softness in your eyes
I watch you doing what you love
—I love you most

A heart full of adventure
A soul I call home
In all these times
—I love you most

◇◆◇ ———— ○ ♣ ○ ———— ◇◆◇

I gave up years of my life
on the idea of love
In the blink of an eye
decades were gone
I tried to love a monster
Now I'm left empty-handed
Rebuilding a life
with all that remains
Trying to remember
that even the darkest night ends
and I will walk out of this chapter

Sometimes the rain falls
hardest on the kindest hearts
It's a beautiful thing
to watch them dance in it

It seems like yesterday
I can hear your voice inside my mind
Your laughter still echoes
through these halls

You left me alone
In a world I can't handle

I don't fit in here
No one knows how to love
I feel so lost
So few are kind

The only comfort that I have
is knowing you're waiting for me
somewhere on the other side

◇◆◇ ━━━━━━ ◦ ♣ ◦ ━━━━━━ ◇◆◇

I gave up trying to be
what you wanted
It was killing me
You wanted to change
and rearrange too many parts of me
You wanted me to be the woman
who lives in your head
You never saw me
Not the real me
You were blinded by society
The love I had to offer
just wasn't enough
I wasn't enough

I never felt whole in your company
I was never able to just be myself
I could feel the judgment
I saw it every time our eyes met
I saw the disappointment
You kept my wings clipped
You thought keeping me small
would keep me close
Over time I stopped feeling anything
Inside I grew dark
I became a shell
My soul just waiting
for my body to catch up
Just waiting for the freedom
that comes with the end

◇◆◇ ━━━━ ∘ ✤ ∘ ━━━━ ◇◆◇

I've lost my way
I'm slowly drowning in my own sorrow
I can't carry your lies, your secrets
I can no longer pretend I'm OKAY
The weight of this is just too much
The smile I've been hiding behind
is fading
With each day that passes
parts of me disappear
I'm tired of hiding you
so you can retie your mask

◇◆◇ ━━━━ ∘ ♣ ∘ ━━━━ ◇◆◇

You come to me on my darkest of days
A gentle breeze to my raging storm
Your soft whispers
silencing the war in my head
You let me in your world
and helped me heal my own
Inside your arms, the nightmares stopped
I found my voice
I began to fight
I fought for the life
they tried to keep me from
You turned chaos to calm
You turned fear into love
Turning my world upside down
in the most beautiful way

I watch the sunrise
so I know a new day is beginning
a fresh start
a clean slate

I watch the sunset
so I know that no matter what happened
tomorrow will come
and give me another chance

A storm is coming
Lightning dances across the walls
Thunder rages in the distance
Tears roll down my face
It's then I realize
Love doesn't live here anymore

It was never really about her, was it?

It was about how she made you feel
and how she made you look
You fed your ego
with the stars in her eyes
Slowly draining
every bit of light from her
And when her shine was gone
you wiped the black from your soul
on her heart and walked away

The only person I owe anything to in this world is me
The woman I neglected
The one I turned my back on
I'm sorry I hurt you
I'm sorry I let them hurt you
I didn't help you chase your dreams
because I didn't believe in you
I'm sorry
I filled your head with doubt
I'm sorry I didn't tell you
that you are beautiful
I never saw your worth
I never made you feel good enough
I let you settle for less
than what you deserved
I am sorry
You deserve the world
and this time
I'm going to help you get it

She lives her life broken
With the best of them
She knows it's not perfect
and neither is she
Love sometimes leaves you
bent and bleeding
and everyone
wasn't meant to stay
She knows sometimes
it's going to rain and rain hard
So she learned how to dance in it

She's tired
Tired of living her life
by someone else's standards
By someone else's definition
of what's important
By someone else's rules

Tired of loving in a world
so full of hate
You are hated
just for being different

A world where parents hurt their children
Where husbands hurt their wives
and everyone pretends not to see a thing

Where people we trust
are the ones that hurt
us the most
This world is exhausting

And it's heartbreaking to know
that this is the only world
many will ever know

◇◆◇ ━━━━ ◦ ❖ ◦ ━━━━ ◇◆◇

On the other side of heaven
I'll wait for you
Just past the burnt-out stars
and broken dreams
Look for me
I'll be there waiting
to welcome you home

Out of all the things
I've seen
and all the places
I've been
Trying to love you
has been my most
dangerous adventure

My past will no longer define me
I am not that woman anymore
This woman won't stand in the corner afraid
While you rage out of control
I won't blame myself for your shortcomings
No, not this woman
This woman will step out of this corner
and take you back to hell
Right where you belong

You claim to be
all Peace, Love, and Light
Truth is
you're more Drama, Bitterness, and Bullshit

I want you to know
you made my life worth living
You made my life beautiful

On the days where life almost
got the best of me
It was your face
that brought me back

I prayed for you
So many prayers
I thought they fell on deaf ears
but you came when I needed you most

You saved me
You continue to save me
Saving me from the insanity within myself

All the pain was nothing
For you, I'd do it a thousand times over
And at the end of my time
when they ask me what I'm most proud of

I will smile, and the answer
will always be the same...
Her

◇◆◇ ———— ○ ✤ ○ ———— ◇◆◇

I don't know
what true peace feels like
I've been in survival mode
for far too long
Always watching
Always waiting
Waiting for the bomb to drop
or the phone to ring
waiting for people to leave
waiting to fall

All I know is hurt
This is the life I have lived
I'm exhausted but can't sleep
I know it's coming
It's just a matter of time
And for me just keeps ticking away

She's all stardust, that one
filled with a magic
not everyone can handle
So if you can't take a little burn
get out of her way

◇◆◇ ━━━━━ ◦ ♣ ◦ ━━━━━ ◇◆◇

Birds flying circles
in the distance
She hears them calling her name
Begging her to spread her wings
Inviting her to play their game

◇◆◇ ━━━━━ ◦ ♣ ◦ ━━━━━ ◇◆◇

I search for you
in every crowd
Looking for eyes so blue
All of your words
I carry with me
Forever lost in memories of you

He was the poetry
I never dreamt of creating
My beautiful sunset
after a raging storm

The autumn wind begins to cry
Blowing through the trees
It's singing that familiar song again
The one that's meant
for only me

I'd give anything to see you
My hands long to touch your face
I don't know where to find you
You're gone
You disappeared without a trace

No one noticed my silence
They all ignored my pain
The cries all went unheard
My mind slowly losing the game

Days and nights in darkness
My tears so often flowed
A heart so heavy from the pain
Stories they would never know

The end has finally come for me
Taking my last fall from grace
Keep my memory with you
I'll be gone without a trace

◇◆◇ ————— ◦ ♣ ◦ ————— ◇◆◇

I always wondered what I looked like
through your eyes
and then you showed me

I saw the mess of a woman I was
I saw a life not worth living
A body not worth loving

I saw a broken soul
and a bleeding heart

I saw someone I didn't know
No sparkle in my eyes
My smile long since faded away

I didn't like the me you saw
So I opened my eyes a little wider
and I walked away

Walking away from you
led me to find myself
The woman in me I had forgotten
I found my voice
I discovered a freedom
I didn't know existed
A freedom that lets me be me
No matter who that is
I can be the woman
with the messy hair
who eats cookies for breakfast
The woman who stays up too late
watching things she shouldn't
I can have unplanned adventures
full of backroads and loud music
I can walk barefoot in the mud
and laugh at stupid jokes
until tears roll down my face
Most importantly, I can say no

So no, you don't get access to this woman
and no, you don't get to hurt me anymore

I've been where you are
Standing on the edge of change
Afraid to move
Afraid not to
Living in silence
The walls around you closing in
Sleepless nights
Praying for someone to come
For someone to hear you
Knowing no one can save you
You have to save yourself
if there was ever a time, it's now
Pick yourself up
As slowly as you need to
Pick yourself up and move
Let the tears fall as you go
Just beyond that edge
is the life you know you deserve
It's waiting for you
Waiting for you to take that first step

◇◆◇ ━━━━━ ∘ ✤ ∘ ━━━━━ ◇◆◇

I never deserved the life you showed me
The fear
The panic
The tears
I deserved a soft place
A place with love and laughter

A shelter from life's storms
You broke everything I believed in
Even myself

When the storm inside me began to rage
I had no choice
but to make you my first casualty
There was no choice if I wanted to survive
and I deserved to live
I wanted to live

I will never apologize for that

In this life, was I loved enough?
Will someone plant flowers at my grave?

Will they come to sit and talk to me?
Tell me the words they could never say

Will their tears fall down softly?
Like a warm summer rain

Can they feel that I am there with them
Please let me take away their pain

I didn't grow up believing in fairytales
I was never waiting for Prince Charming
to come and save me

I knew if I wanted to survive
I had to save myself

I realized young that love was
not butterflies and kind words

Love was often a tear-stained face
and bloodshot eyes

I learned to build walls
so high they blocked my view of the sun
and I slowly withered away
Dreaming wasn't something I could afford to do
Reality kept me broken and grounded

I never learned that loving myself was OKAY
That it was necessary
I was shown all my imperfections
I learned all about my flaws

I was never anyone's blessing
I was my family's sin

Finally
I found meaning in the madness
Never again will I walk alone
My past will no longer haunt me
In your heart
I have found my home

Eyes that feel like home
Hair the color of fire
Quiet like a gentle storm
He's her heart's one desire

He has seen me at my darkest
Through my many shades of pain
he knows all my secrets
All about my hidden shame
He tells me that I'm beautiful
He's convinced me it's my name

In your world, I never mattered
My life was just a game
In darkness, I survived
So darkness I became

All the times I cried alone
Lying in my bed at night
Just wishing that my pain would end
Little did I know, I wished for you

Sitting in the grass watching the sky
Seeing a star fall from grace
Whispering my wish just to be okay
I didn't know it then, but I wished for you

A birthday cake, candles burning bright
I'd close my eyes and blow
Wishing for a life filled with happiness and love
Each passing year, the same wish for you

Every 11:11
Blowing dandelions into the breeze
Tossing a shiny penny down a well
Each one a silent wish
Each one a wish for you

◇◆◇ ——————— ◦✤◦ ——————— ◇◆◇

Staring down the rabbit hole
Should I stay, or should I go
These roads I walk
I walk alone
The world I know
is not my own
Staring down the rabbit hole
Should I stay
or should I go?

I have a mind
most wouldn't understand
Haunted by a past,
I can't remember
Living a life,
I'd rather forget
A heart caught between memories of you

She made her home among the broken
She found comfort with the lost
The souls who understood pain
The ones fighting for a spot

They understood her type of sorrow
the ache that never went away
It wasn't a phase for them
not something they would or
could just get over
They couldn't just move on
This was their life
Their silence said it all
but not everyone had what it took
to hear their words

Maybe I was meant to walk these broken roads
To love broken people
Maybe that was my mission
this time around
To give more than I would ever get
To love hard and absorb the pain
maybe that was meant to be my journey

And maybe the next time I pass
through
I'll find the love I so desperately crave

In every lifetime
I have searched for you
I hoped in this one
we would have gotten it right
But the universe had other plans
and love let us down again

My soul is restless
I was born to run
Playing hide and seek with the moon
Forever chasing the sun

In her eyes
you can see it
the calming of the storm
That day the victim in her died
And the survivor in her was born

Sometimes I think
I'm playing the fool
You're more than I can stand to lose
In this crazy world we live in
My heart belongs to you

And just like that
it was over
The final curtain fell
The devil stood before her
Welcoming her to hell

◇◆◇ ——————— ∘ ♣ ∘ ——————— ◇◆◇

With trembling hands
She found her voice
Silence was no longer
Her color

◇◆◇ ——————— ∘ ♣ ∘ ——————— ◇◆◇

You forgot, didn't you?
Forgot who you were before this started
You waged war on yourself
and never looked back
You are not broken, sweet one
the mirror you look in for approval is dirty
Kept that way by a life you can't escape
by a boy who can't keep up
The flower versus the weed
You are still in there
Somewhere behind the doubt
Let go of what holds you down
Let your Goddess come back out.

You soften the darkness
Your voice
puts my demons to sleep
Inside your arms
I find my respite

Their lips crashed together
A mouthful of sin
He started a battle
A battle he was never going to win

You expected her to give up her entire world
A world she worked so hard to build
To change everything about herself
All for the promise of love
You tried so hard

She saw
the one-sided love you were offering
She knew she was worth more
You failed

I told you
loving me wouldn't be easy
I'm the product
of a dysfunctional type of love
Some of my pieces are broken
some are gone
I go days without seeing the sun
My mind is in total darkness
My soul
wanders aimlessly through the abyss
There are days
when I don't even know who I am
All I can remember is where I came from
and the battles I've fought
Even when I'm here, I'm not
I'm barely surviving
I tried to warn you
I told you to walk away
You stayed
You stayed
and my darkness swallowed you whole

◇◆◇ ━━━━━ ◦ ♣ ◦ ━━━━━ ◇◆◇

I wonder what you see
When your eyes look at me
Is it the little girl you abandoned
or the woman you set free?

Could it be your own hopes
with a few of your own dreams?
Everything you ever wanted
Just out of reach

Maybe it's a little more simple
Tell me--what do you see?
Just a page in your history
or all that you will never be?

It's one of those nights
it's a little too dark
and a little too quiet
The kind of night when reality hits
The kind of night when you realize
nothing will ever be the same

There are many things you learn
while dealing with death
One of the most important
is the reminder to live

Let me color you beautiful
with a touch of darkness
from the moon
Let me show them who you really are
A meadow full of wildflowers
awakening to summer's first bloom

I'll paint the brightest sunrays
In the wild of your hair
In my heart is where I'll carry you
until the day you're finally here

◇◆◇ ──────── ○ ♣ ○ ──────── ◇◆◇

I refuse to reignite the embers
left by the ones that came before me

To feed the ghosts living in your head

I bring to this my own fire
and I plan on burning the bitch down

I shine too bright
to be hidden somewhere
on your list of maybe's

I am consumed by wanderlust
I crave country roads,
longways home,
and you

◇◆◇ ━━━━ ∘ ❖ ∘ ━━━━ ◇◆◇

Surrounded by signs
Drowning in memories

◇◆◇ ━━━━ ∘ ❖ ∘ ━━━━ ◇◆◇

We teach our children
to stay between the lines

As adults, we realize
that survival sometimes comes
from crossing them

I used to battle with my darkness
So afraid to let it win
Today I will surrender
Today I will let my life begin

Tired of feeling broken
Tired of being strong
Tired of living this life
Tired of playing along

Living in the fast lane
Trying to make it through
I don't know where I'm going
All roads lead to you

I don't want to live forever
I can't do this anymore
I let my love rain down
You just close another door

Sometimes I think I'm playing the fool
You're more than I can stand to lose
In this crazy world we live in
My heart belongs to you

I don't know where I'm going
I don't know what to do
You're the one thing that I'm living for
All roads lead to you

◇◆◇ ——————— ◦ ♣ ◦ ——————— ◇◆◇

106

In a world full of darkness
You're the only light I see
The rainbow after my storm
You brought me to life
You set my soul free

Feeling the rain as it starts to fall
Watching the storm light up the sky
Finding the strength inside that I needed
Realizing that even the angels sometimes cry

Let's run away together
Just you and me
We can build a little house
Let's live by the sea

We can frolic and play
In the warm summer sun
We can live like a child
Whose life has just begun

◇◆◇ ━━━━━ ∘ ♣ ∘ ━━━━━ ◇◆◇

I'm just an old soul
trying to survive
in a world that has forgotten

I can feel myself slipping
Deep into the unknown
I can hear the darkness calling
Begging me to come home

Clipped wings regrow
Broken hearts heal
Numbness slowly fades away
We can begin again

Fading back into the darkness
My soul starts to roam
Going back down a broken road
It's the only home I know

Do you think it hurts to die?
Do the angels gather 'round?
Do they feel your pain?
Does it make them cry?
Is someone there waiting
so you don't have to walk alone?
Someone waiting in the darkness
to hold your hand
and walk you home

I miss you most
when the night finally comes
When all the world goes silent
and my day is almost done

The only sound I hear
is the wind crying out your name
that's when it hits me the hardest
things will never be the same

Never again will I see your face
or that sparkle in your eye
You left that without warning
I didn't get to say goodbye

My life is so different
without you, I feel so alone
but I will continue this journey
Until it's my turn to go home

◇◆◇ —————— ∘ ✤ ∘ —————— ◇◆◇

Bent but not broken
I stand alone
My tarnished crown
My splintered throne

Just a faceless pawn
Caught up in your game
I forgot my own strength
I forgot my own name

I may have lost this battle
But I intend to win the war
I'm starting my life over
You have no control anymore

I'm choosing my own destiny
I'm chasing my own dreams
I'm taking back my power
I remembered I'm a Queen

Her heart is pure magic
A true dandelion girl
Give her your love
She'll give you her world

I am deeper
than most care to swim
That's where your illusion stops
and where my truth begins

She's not like the others
She may talk a little too much
because her ears were once deafened by silence
She watches a little too closely
Love once left her blinded
She worries a little more than she should
Those she trusted let her down
Her laughter may carry a little too long
It's to make up for the years filled with tears
She's going to love you a little too much
It's the only way she knows

What would you do
if I just walked away?
Would the world crash around you?
Would the stars begin to fade?

Would it wake up your soul
if I just said goodbye?
I'm tired of ignoring the truth
Tired of living this lie

Little pink roses
A mound of soft dirt
A world left shattered
Indescribable hurt

My heart wasn't ready
I needed you to stay
A part of me died too
The night you went away

In the end
When the lights start to dim
I hope you know I tried

And on your darkest nights
When your memories win
I'll hold you as you cry

The wind of change is blowing
She let her demons go
Along with them went the pain
It was never hers to own

This house is a prison
The walls are closing in
If Satan knocked tomorrow
She'd gladly let him in

The cocoon has been broken
She's spreading her wings
Her season has started
She's moving on to better things

She loved you
A fire inside her blazed out of control
She burned for you
A shattered heart found a way to love
It loved you
You weren't perfect
Perfection wasn't what she was looking for

She wasn't enough, was she?
You kept living in the shadows of the one who hurt you
The one that used you up then spit you out
She paid for that
A price that wasn't hers

She gave up
She needed the sun
The shadows weren't enough
One day it will hit you
You will awaken
The woman you overlooked changed

While you were caught up in the dream of oleander
the wallflower bloomed

◇◆◇ ═══════ ∘ ✣ ∘ ═══════ ◇◆◇

Here I am
I'm still standing
Your actions didn't make me
Your words?
They couldn't break me
Neither could your lies

Your chains bind me
My life is no longer my own
Hateful words remind me
there's no place like home

The crown may be tarnished
and showing signs of war
It may be missing a few stones
but here I am
I'm still standing
Alive and breathing
Surviving on my own

Haunted by a love I never knew
Hidden by a mask of lies
You tried to color yourself pretty
But couldn't stay between the lines

Some days
I feel like I can take on the world
Like I finally stand a chance
Other days
Like today
I wish
it would just swallow me whole

She's a broken mess of chaos
With love in her heart
and the stars in her eyes

I let myself cry today
I cried for a past I'll never forget
One I'm not sure I will ever get over
but I know I can't go back
because I'd never survive

I cried for the adventure
that's waiting for me
The twists and turns
that life brings
For that, I am ready
I am finally ready

I cried for me today
I watched the dawn break
and knew my life was about to change
Getting to live my life by my own rules
and finally understanding
the phrase...Life Is Beautiful

◇◆◇ ━━━━ ∘✤∘ ━━━━ ◇◆◇

I hear you're telling
everyone that will listen
you made me

You made me question my sanity
You filled me with self-doubt
You made me forget who I was
and what I was capable of

Nightmares replaced my dreams
Laughter was replaced by screams

You changed the definition of love for me
You almost broke me

The person I am today
You had no part in making
I put myself back together
Piece by broken piece
I made myself strong

You don't get to know this one

Abuse isn't always
black and blue
Sometimes it's love songs
and roses

It's not always broken bones
and blackened eyes
Sometimes it's a broken spirit
and a battered mind

But he's so nice
are sometimes empty words
giving him time to change
his mask

Sometimes abuse is invisible
to the naked eye
but can be felt right down
to the broken soul

I was more than he could handle
I was a little too strong
a little too brave
a little too loud

The magic in my soul
left a bad taste in his mouth
The fire in my eyes
blinded him

It didn't take him long to realize
my type of wild
would never be tamed

Things aren't always what they seem
He wasn't what he pretended to be

He was hate dressed up as tenderness
A walking fabrication

The warmth is his heart
fueled by rage

His laughter was drenched in jealousy

From his mouth, the lies effortlessly flowed

His eyes. oh those eyes
In those eyes
I thought I saw love
It was only anger in disguise

I gave up on forever
When you showed me
it was more than you could handle

You dangled it in front of me
With empty promises of love
You had a mouthful of pretty words
but a heart
that couldn't back them up

You
let them poison your mind
and I became
your enemy

Instead of building a life together
a war was waged
and you destroyed it

Just when I thought
the battle with my demons was over
you re-laced my gloves

She wanted to run
through a field of wildflowers
The sun warm on her skin
Spending the entire day barefoot
a gentle breeze blowing through her hair

Spending the evening hours
chasing fireflies
only to let them go
Watching them with pure amazement

She missed the days of her childhood
Summers of innocent fun

She missed the days
before the world broke her heart

She'll be the one you think about
The one you can't forget
Years will pass by
Everything will change
She will still be there
Trapped inside your soul
A song on the radio will take you back
A scent so familiar
will send your heart reeling
Your mind will play tricks on you
You will see her face in clouds
You will feel her touch
when you're lying in bed alone
The wind will whisper her name

You let her go
Let her just walk away
and now
she's the one you can't forget

The day will come
When I am no longer

Sit back
Read my words
Feel my love

And know because of you
I grew stronger

◇◆◇ ━━━━━ ∘ ❖ ∘ ━━━━━ ◇◆◇

I got lost in the eyes of a stranger
It was there
I finally found myself

◇◆◇ ━━━━━ ∘ ❖ ∘ ━━━━━ ◇◆◇

You saved me
Not from a world gone mad
or a love gone wrong
No, you saved me
from a life turned black

You are the light
In a mind that races with darkness

You are the strength
In a soul that is full of fear

You are the love
I have longed for

The adventure
I so desperately craved

You
You saved me
You saved me from myself

◇◆◇ ——————— ◦ ♣ ◦ ——————— ◇◆◇

My world without you
such a melancholy place
The music would be silenced
Colors slowly fade away

I would no longer see the moon
The same way as before
I'd drown myself in sorrow
My waves never reaching the shore

Slowly I would disappear
Dwindle to the darkest black
A soul left to wander
A heart that's never coming back

With her heart
tucked safely inside his
She jumped
and she never looked back
Life was waiting

I want to go wild and crazy
I need to set my soul free
I have a longing to be that girl
The girl they said never to be

Meet me here
Where the mountains
kiss the moon
Love me there

The sun will be here soon
Share a dance with me
Let the music guide our hearts

Touch my soul softly
Our bodies are miles apart

Some roads lead to heaven
More roads lead to hell
My road leads to you

Through your strength
I have found my own
In your eyes
I have found my home
With your touch
I begin to feel
Inside your love
I began to heal

◇◆◇ ═══════ ○ ♣ ○ ═══════ ◇◆◇

My pen will speak louder
than my voice ever will

◇◆◇ ═══════ ○ ♣ ○ ═══════ ◇◆◇

You are the soft words
that flow from my pen
chipping away at my walls
Bringing me to life once again

He makes her heart sing
A song so beautifully familiar
It brought them together
and together they danced

Two minds were awakened
Energies out of control
No words to describe it
Two bodies
One soul

◇◆◇ ▬▬▬▬ ∘ ♣ ∘ ▬▬▬▬ ◇◆◇

Blessed is the soul
That falls in love with
a silly heart

◇◆◇ ▬▬▬▬ ∘ ♣ ∘ ▬▬▬▬ ◇◆◇

For you, I tore down my walls
I welcomed you in
I let myself fall

For you, I let myself heal
Mended my broken soul
Allowed my heart to feel

For you, I learned to dance in the rain
Letting the water run over me
Washing away all the pain

For you, I'm shedding this skin
I'm finding myself
Beginning to feel whole again

For you, I want the best version of me
For you, the man that loves me
Loves me for being me

◇◆◇ ────── ○ ✣ ○ ────── ◇◆◇

An empty heart
Tears fill her eyes
Softly humming his favorite lullaby

Memories flood her broken mind
All she wanted
was a little more time
To see his hair
shining in the sun
His life was over
just as it begun

A mother left mourning
A life overcome with sadness
Losing her heart and mind
Forever in melancholy madness

The Love of Lisa—in honor of Danny

The wind is blowing
through the trees
I recognize the song

I know my past is coming for me
It shouldn't be very long

He'll come
and take me by the hand
The tall man
dressed in black

I'll move on to my next life
There will be no turning back

You walking away caused a storm
A storm fueled by pain and anger
The darkest clouds rolled in
The loudest thunder cracked
The heaviest of rain fell

In that storm, I learned who I was
I learned how to survive

In my life, it may rain again
and it may be fierce
but I know that no matter what happens
or how hard that rain falls
I will never drown

More and more often
I visit the darkness
Always waiting
Always wondering
Will today be the day it wins?
Will today be the day I stop fighting?
The whispering in my ear never stops
I hear your words over and over
I'm a haunted house
Your voice the only resident
I remain boarded up, closed off
The light never getting in
I will never have the peace
I so desperately crave
The peace I need to survive

Today I bought myself flowers
I'm realizing my worth
I don't need your validation
to know I'm a good woman
A beautiful woman
Your words will no longer tear me down
Your opinion will no longer cage me
So today, I bought myself flowers
and tomorrow
I just may take over the world

I want real
I want a quiet soul to dream with
Someone to watch the stars with me
Who will eat ice cream at 3am with me
I want lazy days on the couch
and walks in the rain

I need someone to build with
to take a bite out of this world
and make it ours

I want to be taken as I am
Love me when life's good
Love me harder when it's not

Life is too short to be alone
In this darkness
I need someone real

That funny feeling you get
when you finally set your soul free

I'm letting go
I'm going to find freedom in this pain
I'm going to love
Really live
Live a life I used to only dream of
and one day
when I'm ready
One day I will love again

I need to get lost
To go find peace in the mountains
Go listen to the wind sing
through the trees
I want to chase waterfalls
I want to follow them for miles
Feel their power run over me
and heal my aching soul
I need to feel the earth under my feet
Hold mother nature in my hands
I need to recharge my inner battery
Drained by a world of chaos
I need to get lost
or maybe
I need to get found

She let go of a past
that never stopped haunting her

She let go of your opinion
the words you never had the right to say
the words that never rang true

She let go of your broken dreams
and empty promises

She decided to love herself
and she found beauty there

She found her voice
and she followed her dreams

Why him? they asked me
over and over again

Because
he's the only one
that has ever heard my silence

Where seeds of doubt
are planted
insecurities bloom

I never was the mom-cut
and minivan type of woman

I'm more of a hot mess
and a muscle car

I need a road trip
an adventure to cleanse my soul
Beautiful skies above me
Below country road

I loved you with all the love
I should have been giving myself
I gave you the world
While the moon held the sun,
and the stars softly wept

I could set the moon on fire
and you still wouldn't
ask me to dance

The smell of rain is so intoxicating
The scent carried in the breeze
Warning you of his arrival
I just close my eyes
and breathe deep
Filling my lungs with his electricity
Knowing that soon
I will have the chance
to wash away my worries
Even if it's only temporary

◇◆◇ ———— ○ ♣ ○ ———— ◇◆◇

I can feel myself
slipping away
All that was good about me
slowly fading
A mind so full of color
turning to shades of gray

He was gasoline
and she was the flame
They gave each other
the power to destroy
and that's exactly
what they did
Love didn't stand a chance

I need quiet
I need the noise of the world
to just fade away
I need to lose myself
in my daydreams
Chase them into reality
I need to get lost in nature
and just drown the noise out
I need all of this
and I need you

I always pictured my life a little differently
I saw it with a lot more love
I didn't see it with all these battles
Always something to overcome
Another mountain to climb
I never expected an easy road
Maybe one with fewer potholes
I thought I'd have more adventures
See all the beautiful things I've read about
Instead, I spend most days
trying to see the good in myself
Trying to find my worth
Somewhere along this journey, I lost it
Maybe I'll find it
Maybe I won't
I just know I'm tired
and this is all going a little too fast
Just like they said it would
So despite the struggles
life has handed me
The childhood I never had
or never finding the love I crave
I will rise each day
and carry on
with this crazy little life I was given

In another life
We would have been magic
The very definition of love
But in this life
We just couldn't get it right

We watch the same moon
but under different skies

◇◆◇ ——————— ∘ ✣ ∘ ——————— ◇◆◇

Trying to be the beautiful you needed
in your world
left me drowning in mine

◇◆◇ ——————— ∘ ✣ ∘ ——————— ◇◆◇

I crave peace
The type of peace
that comes with closure
I'm letting you go
cutting the last string
between us
I forgive you
but most importantly
I forgive me

Welcome back you
It's been awhile

Nostalgia
hits different when you get older
You find yourself getting lost in thought
over the little things
The things you didn't think mattered back then

I remember evenings
spent on my aunt's porch swing
No conversation in particular
It was just a comfortable place
a safe place

I think about snapping beans
on my Nanny's front porch
Not that I enjoyed the task
It was more the laughter
that filled the air
from the women around me
I have no idea what they found so funny
and I probably wouldn't have wanted to
but oh, that sound

I used to look out my bedroom window at night
and watch the yellow glow under the garage door

I pictured my dad on the other side
doing what he loved
wishing he spent a little more time
inside the house

What I wouldn't give
to talk to him just one more time

I loved to watch the moon as a child
I thought it followed me everywhere
I miss my childhood friend Billie Jo
I wonder where life has taken her
and I pray that it's good
So many thoughts
run through my mind on days like today

I think of my child
a grown woman now
I think of her cheeky smile
and contagious giggle
I remember watching her sleep
and praying for life to be good to her

So many memories flood my mind
So many experiences
It went too fast

Now I'm getting to see
life through the eyes of my granddaughter
Enjoying every little thing

I hope someday a long way down this crazy road
when I am no longer walking it
I hope I filled her life with the little things
that makes nostalgia so amazing

ABOUT THE AUTHOR

Emily James' soul roams from the mountains of Pennsylvania to the mountains of North Carolina. She shares her life with her fiancé Brian, her daughter Kirsten, her son-in-law Gage, and her littlest love, granddaughter Miss Elliott Rose.

You can follow Emily James on both Facebook and Instagram.

facebook.com/akaemilyjames

instagram.com/akaemilyjames

Emily James is also a featured author in two of 300 South Media Groups's anthologies:

Rise From Within
As Darkness Falls